Love God, Love People
The Roadmap for Christian Living

Dennis Craig

Energion Publications
1241 Conference Rd
Cantonment, FL 32533

Copyright © 2025, Dennis Craig. All Rights Reserved.

Unless otherwise indicated, Scripture quotations taken from the Holy Bible, New International Version®, NIV® Copyright © 1973, 1978, 1984, 2011 by Biblica, Inc.® Used by permission of Zondervan. All rights reserved worldwide."

Scripture quotations marked NKJV are taken from the New King James Version®. Copyright © 1982 by Thomas Nelson. Used by permission. All rights reserved.

Cover Image: AI generated by GPT Image and expanded and adapted using Firefly in Photoshop.

ISBN: 978-1-63199-957-4
eISBN: 978-1-63199-958-1

Energion Publications
1241 Conference Rd
Cantonment, FL 32533

energion.com
pubs@energion.com

Table of Contents

Introduction 1
   1. Before it Begins 3
   2. The Beatitudes 7
   3. Salt and Light 13
   4. The Old Testament Was not Written
      with Disappearing Ink 17
   5. Make Sure You Are Comparing Yourself
      to the Right Standard 21
   6. Whether You Sin Is not as Important as
      Whether You Forgive 25
   7. Cut off the bad parts. 29
   8. The Truth Will Set You Free,
      but a Lie Will Ensnare You. 33
   9. You Want Me to Do What? 37

Introduction to Matthew Chapter 6 41
   10. Spiritual Integrity 43
   11. There Is a Right Way to Do Things 47
   12. What Are Your Priorities? 51
   13. God Knows Your Needs 55

Introduction to Matthew Chapter 7 59
   14. First Things First 61
   15. It Really Is not Complicated 65
   16. Things Are not Always What They Seem 71
   17. Location, Location, Location 77
   18. All Authority 83

One Last Word from the Author… 87

Introduction

Let me start out by admitting something to you, my reader – I have read the Bible many times, but I am in no way a Biblical scholar. I have been in church since the age of four, and as a result I have heard thousands of sermons in my life. Since the age of twenty-two I have been in ministry of some kind – both as a volunteer and as a profession.

The result of these years in churches and ministry is that I love to hear, sing, and speak His Word. I love every scripture, and I take to heart 2 Timothy 3:16 which tell us, "All Scripture is God-breathed and is useful for teaching, rebuking, correcting and training in righteousness."

This book is born out of the past three months of my life. I will be transparent and share with you that recently I have gone through a time of spiritual difficulty and strife. A ministry which I was heavily involved in fell apart and I could do nothing to stop it from happening. I lost friendships which I thought would last and lost a church home that had become what I believed to be family. I was broken spiritually. As someone who has attended church since the age of four and been involved in Christian ministry since I graduated college at twenty-two, I was at a place I had never been before. I wondered if I had gotten it wrong the entire time. I was angry at God, my former pastor, and the friends who I felt had casually cast me aside. Most of all I was angry with myself.

I do not know if you have ever been where I found myself. I thought I knew what living the Christian life was all about. I thought that I knew how churches were "supposed' to work and how we were "supposed" to love and impact the people around us. So, where did everything go so horribly wrong?

As I was soul-searching, I began reading Matthew 5 through 7 and found that I could not stop. God continuously led me back to it over and over and revealed things to me with every single verse.

What I realized while reading these chapters is that the entire heart of Jesus' ministry on earth was written here. It is an instruction manual for the Christian life. He was giving the children of God a literal roadmap to finding His heart and to bringing the Father's Kingdom to the world. To making it "on earth as it is in heaven." He was breaking down the barriers that have existed between God and man from the beginning. Even more than that, He gave us the keys to breaking down the barriers we have created between each other.

These chapters breathed life into dry bones. These chapters changed my heart in an unbelievable way. These chapters brought me back to a place where I felt I could again serve the God who died for me and loves me.

I kept writing note after note and decided if God meant for me to do something with it, I better get started. This book is that something.

I guess the best way to describe the following pages is about forty percent bible study and 60 percent commentary. It is everything that God revealed to my heart over the past few months of my life because it brought me out of a place of real doubt and fear to a place of absolute peace and light. My hope is that it can do the same for you.

Grace and Peace,
Dennis

1. Before it Begins

> *"Jesus went throughout Galilee, teaching in their synagogues, proclaiming the good news of the kingdom, and healing every disease and sickness among the people. News about him spread all over Syria, and people brought to him all who were ill with various diseases, those suffering severe pain, the demon-possessed, those having seizures, and the paralyzed; and he healed them. Large crowds from Galilee, the Decapolis, Jerusalem, Judea and the region across the Jordan followed him."*
> (Matthew 4:23-25)

Jesus had ended His temptation in the wilderness where He defeated Satan by the power of God's Word. He then called His disciples and began traveling throughout the entire region, demonstrating God's power and teaching about the Kingdom.

He did not go around proclaiming Himself messiah and His equality with God yet. He started by teaching, proclaiming, healing, and demonstrating.

I am about to say something that may upset some of you…. Jesus did all of it with ulterior motives.

He gave sight to the blind, but He did not do it for the blind man.

He made the lame walk, but He did not do it for the lame man.

He freed the demon-possessed, but not for the benefit of the demon-possessed.

He performed these signs and wonders and miracles, and He made sure that people saw them for one reason ... .so that the people would be drawn to GOD. He was not chasing fame or fortune. He was showing the entire purpose of His earthly ministry – to bring the Kingdom of Heaven to earth in word and action.

He drew all to himself, and it showed as crowds began to gather and follow Him wherever He went. He saw these crowds and knew it was time to proclaim the mysteries of God to the people He loved.

Many people miss it. Did you? He performed the miracles to draw attention to God and to bring people in. The miracles were a demonstration of the power that GOD had given Him, so when He spoke, they would listen in. The miracles were not the ultimate purpose, they created an opening for the message of God to come through. The miracles were not the focus, they were simply the preamble to the sermon which He was about to deliver, and we are about to study in the following chapters.

So, let me ask you… what is your ulterior motive?

I hear people all the time asking why their prayers are not answered. Why didn't God heal me? Why will God not bless me financially? Why hasn't the Holy Spirit given me this or that gift? What this chapter of scripture tells me is that if we are not receiving the blessings of God, our motives may not be correct. Are we asking for the healing to simply be healed, or are we asking so that God is glorified through the healing? Are we wanting a financial blessing just for ourselves, or are we asking for a financial blessing to bless others and help to build the Kingdom? Do we desire the fire of the Holy Spirit to simply look more spiritual and feel the "goosebumps" or do we desire for that manifestation to draw others to repentance and to give glory to God?

I pray we as a church and as Christians will begin to search for our ulterior motive. I pray that we will stop chasing the fireworks of miracles and manifestations and realize that it is all intended to draw us closer to **Him** so that we can hear God's Word and let it bring us to a greater understanding of who God is, and who we can be through Him. Jesus lets us know that if we seek first the Kingdom of God and His righteousness all that other stuff (miracles, etc.) will come. The key is seeking Him first, now, and always.

NOTES

2. The Beatitudes

"Blessed are the poor in spirit, for theirs is the kingdom of heaven. Blessed are those who mourn, for they will be comforted. Blessed are the meek, for they will inherit the earth. Blessed are those who hunger and thirst for righteousness, for they will be filled. Blessed are the merciful, for they will be shown mercy. Blessed are the pure in heart, for they will see God. Blessed are the peacemakers, for they will be called children of God. Blessed are those who are persecuted because of righteousness, for theirs is the kingdom of heaven.

Blessed are you when people insult you, persecute you and falsely say all kinds of evil against you because of me. Rejoice and be glad, because great is your reward in heaven, for in the same way they persecuted the prophets who were before you." (Matthew 5:3-12)

I have read these verses hundreds of times in my forty-nine years of life, and tonight something hit me which had never occurred to me before. These nine steps show the process of what occurs when we follow Christ and receive the Spirit of God. They are the roadmap to the heart of Jesus. They are the arc of the Christian life.

The first three beatitudes describe people who are lacking something. Are you the single parent struggling to make ends meet and losing hope? Have you lost someone or something and find yourself unable to pull yourself out of the sorrow of that loss? Are you the person who is scared to step forward or speak out because of the fear of rejection? Those first three beatitudes speak directly to you and are intended to show you the Lord will provide what you are lacking.

So many people consider being meek or in mourning or poor in Spirit as being in a place of weakness. When we are in these circumstances, we see those around us who walk in boldness or have joy as being so much stronger than we are. Jesus wants us to know that each of these positions is a position where we can receive. It is a position of POTENTIAL!

Physicists show us that there is a stark difference between potential and kinetic energy. Kinetic energy is when we are in motion, but potential energy is independent of the environment. It is energy that we hold within ourselves, and it can easily turn into kinetic energy when we change position, state, or composition.

When we are meek, in mourning, or poor in spirit we are in the perfect position for the Holy Spirit to come in and CHANGE OUR COMPOSITION. That is what Holy Spirit does! He is a catalyst for change. He comes in and re-makes from the inside out. He wants to strengthen what is meek, give joy to the mourning, and fill us with more of His Spirit than we ever thought we could contain.

Then, Jesus gives us the fourth of the beatitudes, which I strongly believe is the most important one. Those that hunger and thirst for righteousness, you will be FILLED! What you are missing in your life will not EVER be filled by the things of this world. John 4:13 tells us "Jesus answered, 'Everyone who drinks this water will be thirsty again, but whoever drinks the water I give them will never thirst. Indeed, the water I give them will become in them a spring of water welling up to eternal life.'")

People who are hungry eat food. People who are thirsty drink water. People who have emptiness and hunger in their spirit constantly seek to fill that emptiness with the things of this world but are never truly successful. You must hunger and thirst for righteousness and the things of God to truly be filled. No alcohol, drug, food, or pleasure of the flesh will ever fill the emptiness in your life. Only Jesus my friends...only Jesus.

This hunger and thirst will lead us to doing those things which embolden and strengthen our spiritual walk. An associate of mine has stated that spiritual discipline is evidenced by the daily application of three important principles – prayer, worship, and Word. Hungering and thirsting after God makes these three things an absolute necessity in the life of a believer.

When we devote time to prayer, worship, and the Word it satisfies us in a way we have never experienced before. When we begin to explore the unbelievable blessings which await us in these disciplines and the Holy Spirit begins to replace the emptiness we feel inside, we cannot get enough. We hunger for more of Jesus.

When we finally begin to realize our potential in Christ and begin to satisfy the hunger in our souls with God's word it leads us directly to the last of the beatitudes. These last three beatitudes describe people who have been filled by God and who have begun to show themselves as followers of Jesus not only through words but actions as well. They show evidence of the change in their heart by showing mercy, making peace, and a purity of heart towards all men.

I do not believe this is an accident. People come to the Lord poor in spirit, meek, and mourning. They begin to hunger and thirst for righteousness and God fills them. Once they are filled with his Spirit, they begin to exhibit the fruits of His Spirit which results in them showing mercy and making peace. The Beatitudes are the Christian experience laid out for us. A journey from empty to full......from dark to light.... from mourning to dancing.

Now this last part does not really sound all that appealing but is nonetheless true. Matthew 5:10-12 *"Blessed are those who are persecuted because of righteousness, for theirs is the kingdom of heaven. Blessed are you when people insult you, persecute you and falsely say all kinds of evil against you because of me."*

One of the biggest problems that plagues the minds of new Christians is: Why do bad things happen to good people? Jesus lets us know clearly that we will experience persecution and hardship no matter how pure in heart we are or how much mercy and peace we sow. We are never promised an easy life. In fact, Jesus tells us in John 16:33 *"In this world you will have trouble. But take heart! I have overcome the world."* When we begin to demonstrate the love of Christ in a world that rejected Him, we WILL be persecuted against, and lied to, and hated…all for the sake of Jesus.

I need to offer a little warning here – there is an enormous difference between persecution and loss of privilege. When we are challenged because our behavior has not been very Christ-like, or we lose what we feel is a right (when it is merely a privilege) this is not persecution. Too often as Christians, we behave in entitled and arrogant ways rather than realizing that at no point did Jesus ever turn to those who were persecuting him and say, "How dare you treat me like this! Why do I have to walk around all the time? Will these sick and lost people ever stop needing stuff? Do you people realize who I am and what I am going to do for you? How dare you?" No, He loved them and loved them and kept on loving them by dying for their sins.

I know that sometimes it feels like the pain and trouble will last forever, but it is only just a moment. Hold on – here comes the good news. 2 Corinthains 4:17-18 *"For our light and momentary troubles are achieving for us an eternal glory that far outweighs them all. So, we fix our eyes not on what is seen, but on what is unseen, since what is seen is temporary, but what is unseen is eternal."* Those that endure through the times of lack and mourning to be filled with the righteousness of Christ and show the fruits of the Spirit can rejoice - because GREAT IS YOUR REWARD. Even during trials, you are rewarded, and that reward is eternal.

Romans 5:3-4 tells us, *"Not only so, but we also glory in our sufferings, because we know that suffering produces perseverance; perseverance, character; and character, hope."* That hope is the ultimate reward for those who persevere to the end.

See, when Jesus gave us the Beatitudes, he gave us a way out of where we were to where we could be. They are a roadmap that begins with meekness and mourning and ends with an eternal reward. It is the journey for all who call on His name – and the ending is beyond anything we can imagine.

NOTES

3. Salt and Light

> *"You are the salt of the earth; but if the salt loses its flavor, how shall it be seasoned? It is then good for nothing but to be thrown out and trampled underfoot by men. You are the light of the world. A city that is set on a hill cannot be hidden. Nor do they light a lamp and put it under a basket, but on a lampstand, and it gives light to all who are in the house. Let your light so shine before men, that they may see your good works and glorify your Father in heaven."* (Matthew 5:13-16 NKJV)

Being one of the chosen of God is a calling not only to live a life of faith – it is to be SET APART. In John 17:14-16, Jesus is praying for his disciples and declares that *"I have given them Your word; and the world has hated them because they are not of the world, just as I am not of the world. I do not pray that You should take them out of the world, but that You should keep them from the evil one. They are not of the world, just as I am not of the world."*

This is often a huge point of conflict in conversations regarding living the Christian life. Does being a Christian mean that we must avoid sinners or the places where sin is practiced? Can we have dinner at a sports bar if they serve alcohol there? What about if we are invited to a party where people are drinking and smoking? What if we want to go out with friends and sing karaoke but the only place that offers it is filled with drunk people? (The one is personal since I LOVE to sing karaoke)

Jesus does not ask us to separate ourselves completely from the lost of this world, because then we would not be able to further the Kingdom of God by helping the lost find their way back to the Father. How can we reach the lost if we never encounter them? We cannot be the hands and feet of Jesus if they just shut themselves off from the people around them. Jesus ate dinner with tax collectors, prostitutes, and sinners.

However, most of them did not leave the table in the same condition they came. Jesus led them to see their sin and WANT to change. He loved them because He created them and knew that they were more than their sin. They were His children, and He wanted them back. Jesus loved people so much He was willing to die for them, and that kind of love must change how we interact with people. It changes how we think about them, speak to them, and accept them – sins and all. He never forced a change. Jesus knew that people cannot do better until they know better, and that His example would be the best teaching tool ever. We can love like Jesus does and flavor the world around us just as salt flavors food.

However, just as salt stands out for its ability to flavor food and to preserve it – Jesus asks us to STAND OUT by the impact we can have on others by exhibiting the love of Christ. Yes, he sat down with sinners, but he did not partake in their sin…he STOOD OUT. If we looked and acted like everyone else, how would anyone be able to trust in the change which has taken place within us? And, if they cannot trust the change within us, then why would they believe that Jesus could change them? Stand out and show those around you that the change within you is real.

Now, let us discuss being the light of the world. Many Christians like to talk about the light shining within them. They like to describe themselves as being on fire for Christ. However, a warning to all my on-fire brothers and sisters…

Being a light to the world can come with profound responsibility. If you are indeed that city which is set on a hill, then EVERYONE CAN SEE YOU. So, if your light dims, breaks, falters, moves, changes, or darkens then ALL CAN SEE. Lighthouses require constant maintenance. A caretaker is living in the lighthouse twenty-four hours a day, seven days a week and when all around it is dark, that is when the caretaker must be the most vigilant.

We must constantly work and push in to be more like Jesus to make sure our light does not dim. When we place ourselves on a hill, we need to be aware that we have placed ourselves in a place of scrutiny and be prepared to have every aspect of that light watched and judged. I am speaking to those in leadership – Pastors, Teachers, Prophets, Evangelists, and Apostles. If you claim this calling from God in your life, you must be willing to do all you can to maintain your light, because if you fall – everyone can see and be impacted by the change in your light.

I have often described working in the ministry as an invitation to live in a fishbowl. Whether you like it or not, people are watching every aspect of your life. The only difference is that people usually are not watching the fish and hoping it fails. People will actively be watching every moment to see if you have lost your flavor or if your light has dimmed even for a minute so they can shout, "See! I told you it was all a lie."

Is it fair…. no. Is it right…. no. It is just the way it is.

I am not saying you must be perfect. I am not saying you are not allowed to make a mistake. I am saying that you need to be constantly aware that your witness extends far beyond the pulpit or the platform. It reaches to what is on your television, what you post on social media, and even what you may say in the most casual of conversations. Being the light to a darkened world simply means that there is no OFF switch.

Keep your batteries charged by constantly being plugged into the Word. Keep yourself charged by spending time in the secret place worshipping and connecting with the Giver of all light. Keep yourself charged by communicating in prayer with the One who made you. Keep yourself charged – and then shine on my friend. Shine on.

NOTES

4. The Old Testament Was not Written with Disappearing Ink

> *"Do not think that I came to destroy the Law or the Prophets. I did not come to destroy but to fulfill. For assuredly, I say to you, till heaven and earth pass away, one jot or one tittle will by no means pass from the law till all is fulfilled. Whoever therefore breaks one of the least of these commandments, and teaches men so, shall be called least in the kingdom of heaven; but whoever does and teaches them, he shall be called great in the kingdom of heaven."* (Matthew 5:17-19 NKJV)

I was recently in a discussion with a friend about grace and forgiveness. I pointed out that yes, Christ had died for all sinners, but that our sins still carried the penalty of death. "Yes, but that's Old Testament stuff – I'd rather just focus on the grace and forgiveness." As soon as he had said it, I had to stop myself from reacting physically. It was the spiritual equivalent of nails on a chalkboard. I hear it so much from Christians today – and honestly, it scares me.

Jesus was clear regarding His relationship with the Old Testament. He did not come to destroy the law and prophets, but to fulfill them. What does this mean? Well, the Old Testament and old covenant were written as a pact between God and the patriarchs of the faith such as Abraham, Isaac, and Jacob. He promised to grow their descendants into a mighty nation and then gave them the law through Moses. The Israelites were to worship God alone and He would bless them. One of the basic tenets of these laws was that sins could be atoned for by the shedding of blood from a spotless sacrifice. Hebrews 9:22 says, *"In fact, the law requires that nearly everything be cleansed with blood, and without the shedding of blood there is no forgiveness."* The first theme of the Old Testament is atonement from sins.

See, God cannot stand sin. He cannot be around it. Adam and Eve had the pleasure of living in the very presence and glory of God. Then, after the fall, they could not look upon Him anymore. There was a separation.

First through laws, then judges, then Kings, and then prophets, God continued to try repeatedly to give His people a way to reconnect with Him. Man walked in the garden with God in the cool of the day, and ever since then God has desired for us to walk with Him yet again. The second theme of the Old Testament is simple – restoration.

In Jeremiah 31:33-34, God says through the prophet, "This is the covenant I will make with the people of Israel after that time,' declares the Lord. 'I will put my law in their minds and write it on their hearts. I will be their God, and they will be my people. No longer will they teach their neighbor, or say to one another, "Know the Lord," because they will all know me, from the least of them to the greatest,' declares the Lord. 'For I will forgive their wickedness and will remember their sins no more'" See the law did not change. It just went from stone tablets to flesh. It imprints on our hearts when we submit to our Lord.

Christ fulfilled this ultimate purpose of the law and prophets. By His death and resurrection, he bridged the gap again between God and man to allow men to truly know God again and have Him dwell within them. Ultimately, He did two things which will never change:

His willingness to be sacrificed for all sins for all times pays the punishment and penalty for every one of the laws. He shed innocent blood and stood as that spotless sacrifice which was required. He provided the ultimate **atonement** for sin.

His sacrifice meant that all now have access once again to the Father. At the moment of Jesus' death, the veil which separated the Holy of Holies in the temple was torn in two from top to bottom. No longer did we have to rely on a High Priest or Pharisee to function as mediator for us. We could come to God directly and communicate directly with the Creator of the universe. He gave all of us **restoration** to God.

Jesus did not erase the Old Testament - He fulfilled it in every way. The reality of the New Testament and new covenant is that they take the old and make the impossible possible through the life, death, and resurrection of Christ. It shows us just how blessed we really are, how far we have come, and how much we can continue to grow now that the Holy Spirit lives within us.

NOTES

5. Make Sure You Are Comparing Yourself to the Right Standard

> *"For I say to you, that unless your righteousness exceeds the righteousness of the scribes and Pharisees, you will by no means enter the kingdom of heaven."* (Matthew 5:20 NKJV)

Entire churches have broken apart over whether it is faith or works that gets us into heaven. Jesus speaks clearly here that our righteousness needs to exceed the scribes and Pharisees. These groups were known at that time as those who depended on merely following the law to stand in righteousness. I cannot speak for anyone else, but it tells me that being righteous goes BEYOND just following rules and laws.

I looked up the definition of "righteous" and it states, "the quality of being morally right or justifiable."

So often, we judge right and wrong by the world's standard because it is easier. That way, our own wants and needs can factor in and we can move the goalposts into a more favorable position for ourselves. However, the fact is that we need to realize we do not get to be the judge of what is right and wrong. The Bible shows us that it is God and God alone that is the ultimate arbiter of what is right and wrong. Who can live to that standard? Compared to the absolute authority of God, who can count themselves righteous?

When I was a youth pastor, my students continually asked me why bad things happen to good people. My answer never failed to confuse, and sometimes anger, them. My answer was, and remains, "Bad things happen to good people because there are no good people." The Word tells us in Romans 3:10 that "*There is no one righteous, not even one; there is no one who understands; there is no one who seeks God. All have turned away, they have together become worthless; there is no one who does good, not even one*" Whew! I know that sounds harsh, but the truth often does.

There is no bigger sin than the other, and because all of us have sinned, we cannot be called good. The only "good" person who ever walked the planet was Jesus, and if God allowed his suffering, why do we think that our lives would be without pain? Jesus tells us that even His followers will experience pain and persecution!

Here is a difficult thought - on your own, you have absolutely no hope of being counted righteous no matter how well you know the scriptures or follow the "rules." Doing those things does not make you "righteous" – it just means that you have a lot in common with the Pharisees.

So, how do we separate ourselves? How can we be different than the Pharisees? The Pharisees followed the law but refused to follow Christ. We do the one thing that the Pharisees never did - we rely on Jesus. We lean-in whole-heartedly to Him and His gift of salvation. I recently read an article that Righteousness in the eyes of God includes our "character (nature), conscience (attitude), conduct (action), and command (words)." The righteousness of God comes through in all the areas of our world – not just one or the other. But here is the best part, we do not have to rely only on OUR character, conscience, conduct, and command. We have the example of Christ!

We cling to HIS character, HIS conscience, HIS conduct, and HIS command. That is the only way. Align ourselves with the righteousness of Christ and HE will make us righteous!

That is the key to the Kingdom.

NOTES

6. Whether You Sin Is not as Important as Whether You Forgive

"You have heard that it was said to the people long ago, 'You shall not murder, and anyone who murders will be subject to judgment.' But I tell you that anyone who is angry with a brother or sister will be subject to judgment. Again, anyone who says to a brother or sister, 'Raca,' is answerable to the court. And anyone who says, 'You fool!' will be in danger of the fire of hell. "Therefore, if you are offering your gift at the altar and there remember that your brother or sister has something against you, leave your gift there in front of the altar. First go and be reconciled to them; then come and offer your gift. "Settle matters quickly with your adversary who is taking you to court. Do it while you are still together on the way, or your adversary may hand you over to the judge, and the judge may hand you over to the officer, and you may be thrown into prison. Truly I tell you, you will not get out until you have paid the last penny." (Matthew 5:21-26)

It always amazes me when people compare sin. When people of all spiritual levels say, "well, yes I am a sinner, but at least I'm not as bad as that guy." Murder, anger towards your brother, calling someone a "fool": it is simple. It is all the same.

Here is why - sin is separation from God. Anything we do that is outside of God's will separates us from Him. Being separated is the worst part of it. The judgement, hell, or whatever else you want to think of cannot compare to being separated from God.

As soon as you cut the branch from a tree it begins to die. Take fruit off the vine and it is the beginning of the end. Cut off a finger and it will decay and rot. This happens because you are removing it from the very thing that is giving it nourishment and life. When we are separated from God, the result is the same.

And none of us are righteous. None are "clean" of our own selves. All of us, if left to our own devices, face that separation. When Christ was on the cross, His greatest moment of agony came when all our sins fell upon Him and the Father had to turn His back and separate Himself from His son. It was a punishment worse than crucifixion. Think about THAT for a minute.

To overcome this, as said in the previous section of this book, God sent His Son to die as atonement so we could be forgiven of those sins. Forgiveness bridges the separation of sin. Forgiveness is more powerful than sin – more powerful than death.

A lack of forgiveness in your heart can create a separation just as easily as sin. Mark 11:25 says, "And when you stand praying, if you hold anything against anyone, forgive them, so that your Father in heaven may forgive you of your sins."

When we accept Christ as our Savior, we receive the gift of the Holy Spirit. In Matthew 7, Jesus tells us we will be known for our fruits. The Spirit within us gives us the ability to act in the fruits of love, joy, peace, etc. Because of this, we can forgive sins whether we believe we can or not. Simply put – If God forgave us of our sins, we should then forgive others. Once we have received release and peace from our own transgressions, we can take those steps to give that same peace and release to others.

Jesus once told His disciples in John 15:13-17, "Greater love has no one than this: to lay down one's life for one's friends. You are my friends if you do what I command. I no longer call you servants, because a servant does not know his master's business. Instead, I have called you friends, for everything that I learned from my Father I have made known to you. You did not choose me, but I chose you and appointed you so that you might go and bear fruit—fruit that will last—and so that whatever you ask in my name the Father will give you. This is my command: Love each other."

What better way to show your love and to obey His commandments than to lay down your life, desires, wants, needs, pride, and hurt and forgive those who have wronged you. You want to truly be a follower of Christ's way then forget climbing on your soapbox or climbing up on the cross and instead, forgive.

NOTES

7. Cut off the bad parts.

"You have heard that it was said to those of old, 'You shall not commit adultery.' But I say to you that whoever looks at a woman to lust for her has already committed adultery with her in his heart. If your right eye causes you to sin, pluck it out and cast it from you; for it is more profitable for you that one of your members perish, than for your whole body to be cast into hell. And if your right hand causes you to sin, cut it off and cast it from you; for it is more profitable for you that one of your members perish, than for your whole body to be cast into hell." (Matthew 5:27-30)

The other evening, I was relaxing with my family, and we were choosing what movie or show to watch. While browsing the titles, I found myself growing sadder by the minute. Finding a movie or show without sex, violence, foul language, or perversion is almost impossible. We had to resort to a DVD of a movie we all had seen a hundred times simply to protect our kids.

We are bombarded from all sides by images, advertisements, and a society that shoves physical beauty and sexual images of all kinds at us non-stop. We can turn our eyes from one thing without the very next thing being just as offensive as the first. We also fool ourselves into thinking that it is just entertainment and cannot harm us.

Jesus tells us if it is our eye letting in the sin that offend us, we should gouge it out. Do I believe that Jesus gave this as a literal message, of course not. We would have an entire world of half-blind people if he meant it.

Jesus is telling us that if there is a part of our world that we know leads us to temptation or encourages sin that we are to remove it from our lives. I do not know about you but OUCH!

One of the biggest problems is that most people compartmentalize our lives. Church, work, home, friends. We act differently depending on who we are around and what situation we are in. Sometimes we must realize that we need to REMOVE parts of our world to get closer to Christ. We need to take away those things, places, and people that lead us to temptation and sin.

I have heard the argument – "I am the only good influence in their life. I am going to win their soul for God." Some have used this excuse to extend toxic friendships and to date or marry non-Christians. "Missionary relationships" as I call it do not work. Have you ever tried to pull someone up to the top of a ladder from the top? You being pulled off the ladder and crashing to the ground is a much more likely result.

I was leading a Bible study one evening to a group of ladies who were a part of a residential drug treatment program. We were discussing that one of the pieces in recovery is cutting yourself off from the people and circumstances that led you to a place of addiction and one of the ladies said, "But, what if it is your own family?" My response was short and seemed harsh.

"Then, get a new family."

In my previous study "Walking Together: Steps to Discipleship" one of the chapters is titled *Welcome to the Family*. It explains that anyone who calls on the name of the Lord is now a member of a family that is so big it is beyond measure. That family will lift you up and make you stronger in the things of God. You already have that new family so claim it! I know that it is hard to remove people from your life who have been a part of it for as long as you can remember, but if there is even a minute possibility that going back to those circumstances will lead you farther from God – do not do it.

I hate it, but I have had to remove friends and even family from my life because I have come to the hardest realization that my interaction with them encourages me to sin. Anything that stands in between me and a closer relationship with the One who died for me has no place in my world. I do not have the ability to save ANYONE. I can pray for them and continually hope that God reaches into their world, but my personal relationship with Christ and my life as a witness is of much greater value.

Yes, it will hurt but cast them away. There is nothing that you will remove from yourself that God will not replace a hundred-fold.

NOTES

8. The Truth Will Set You Free, but a Lie Will Ensnare You.

> *"Again, you have heard that it was said to the people long ago, 'Do not break your oath, but fulfill to the Lord the vows you have made.' [34] But I tell you, do not swear an oath at all: either by heaven, for it is God's throne; [35] or by the earth, for it is his footstool; or by Jerusalem, for it is the city of the Great King. [36] And do not swear by your head, for you cannot make even one hair white or black. [37] All you need to say is simply 'Yes' or 'No'; anything beyond this comes from the evil one."* (Matthew 5:33-37)

I have one rule in my family, and my kids can tell you what it is with no hesitation, "Whatever you do, don't lie." I cannot stand lying. I know that one sin does not outweigh the other, but lying just infuriates me. My kids absolutely know that if they tell the truth, whatever punishment they may receive will be drastically reduced.

The problem is that lying is an absolutely INTENTIONAL act. No one can say they had no choice but to lie, because it is an absolute choice to deceive someone. I can walk through any truth. Nothing anyone could tell me would be so horrible that I would walk away from them for any reason. If someone is my brother or sister, there is nothing that they could do or say which would make me turn my back on them. But once trust is gone, it is the hardest thing to bring back. I realize that my intense feelings towards lying is something I need to work on and a weakness in my own walk with how harshly I react to lying, but the Word speaks to this truth, "let your yes be yes and your no be no."

The sad thing is how easy it is to lie. We have even come up with the phrase "little white lie" to fool ourselves into thinking that there are some lies which will not hurt us. We convince ourselves that we are not really hurting others when we lie. In fact, we say we are lying to protect their feelings. I've yet to meet a person that thanked me for lying to them. There is not one situation in the world that is IMPROVED by lying. It always makes the circumstance worse in the long run.

If you think I hate lying, you should see what God's Word has to say about it!!!

In Proverbs 6:16-19 it tells us that "There are six things the Lord hates, seven that are detestable to him: haughty eyes, a lying tongue, hands that shed innocent blood, a heart that devises wicked schemes, feet that are quick to rush into evil, a false witness who pours out lies and a person who stirs up conflict in the community."

John 8:44 – "You belong to your father, the devil, and you want to carry out your father's desires. He was a murderer from the beginning, not holding to the truth, for there is no truth in him. When he lies, he speaks his native language, for he is a liar and the father of lies."

Lying is so against the nature of God that he DETESTS IT! Jesus tells us that when we lie, we are speaking the native language of the Devil, who is the father of lies.

Stop making promises based on things of heaven or earth, for it all belongs to the Lord. Make the decision today to keep your word. Remember that lying is a choice! You can also choose to walk in truth. You can choose today to always be truthful – even when it hurts. The bible tells us in Ephesians 4:15-16, "*Instead, speaking the truth in love, we will grow to become in every respect the mature body of him who is the head, that is, Christ. From him the whole body, joined and held together by every supporting ligament, grows, and builds itself up in love, as each part does its work."* Make the words you say and the life you live be a testament to the truth with everything you do so that you can grow in every respect the body of Christ. As a wise old preacher said, "Let your walk match your words, and let your words match the heart of God."

NOTES

9. You Want Me to Do What?

"You have heard that it was said, 'Eye for eye, and tooth for tooth.' But I tell you, do not resist an evil person. If anyone slaps you on the right cheek, turn to them the other cheek also. And if anyone wants to sue you and take your shirt, hand over your coat as well. If anyone forces you to go one mile, go with them two miles. Give to the one who asks you, and do not turn away from the one who wants to borrow from you.

You have heard that it was said, 'Love your neighbor and hate your enemy.' But I tell you, love your enemies and pray for those who persecute you, that you may be children of your Father in heaven. He causes his sun to rise on the evil and the good and sends rain on the righteous and the unrighteous. If you love those who love you, what reward will you get? Are not even the tax collectors doing that? And if you greet only your own people, what are you doing more than others? Do not even pagans do that? Be perfect, therefore, as your heavenly Father is perfect."
(Matthew 5:38-48)

Have you ever had someone ask you to do something that made absolutely no sense? It could be simple, like the belief that drinking a glass of water upside-down will stop your hiccups or putting a wooden spoon over a pot of boiling water will stop it from overflowing. The funny thing about these two popular "old wives' tales" is that when I tried them…. they worked.

People do not always have the right perspective when they face challenges. Far too often they return to what they have always done

– the old ways. The thing most people do not realize is that it is usually their old ways of thinking, speaking, and acting which will make problems much worse. An old phrase tells us that the definition of insanity is doing the same thing repeatedly and expecting a different result. I have always said it this way, "Do what you have always done, and you'll get what you have always got."

A true change often is only accomplished by a change of heart and perspective. It is hard for us to understand just how mind-blowing what Jesus said in these verses was. Loving our enemies? Praying for those who persecute us? Letting someone slap us again once they have done it the first time? This was completely against everything the Jews desired at the time.

When Christ came, Israel had been under oppression for centuries. The Jews had begged for a messiah who would ride in and slaughter the Romans. They demanded a conqueror because they had been conquered and that is what they understood. They demanded vengeance because that was their way of thinking. What they did not understand was that throughout their history, violence only created more violence.

Jesus was directly speaking to the hearts of a nation when he gave the verses above. He showed them that until they could show love and forgiveness even to those that were oppressing them, they were no better than those very people. In fact, to be considered true children of the Father, we must go against what seems justified by our flesh and begin acting out of Spirit.

In our flesh, there is no way we will be able to accomplish the change of perspective that Jesus is outlining for us because when things do not make sense to us, we tend to rebel against it. It is only by allowing ourselves to lean into the Spirit's influence on our lives that we can finally start seeing the truth in what seems foolish. 1 Corinthians 3:18-19 states that "*Stop deceiving yourselves. If you think you are wise by this world's standards, you need to become a fool to be truly wise. For the wisdom of this world is foolishness to God.* "

The part of the verse that speaks to my heart the most is the portion that reads, "*If anyone forces you to go one mile, go with them two miles.*" It was a widespread practice during these times for Roman soldiers to force Jewish citizens to carry their weapons, shields, helmets etc. for one mile. Jews had no choice but to comply. Jesus was telling them that not only should they follow the law, but to show that their character and heart went BEYOND the law. That even oppression, anger, and fear would not stop them from showing a character born out of a change of heart and perspective.

Anyone who has ever drawn breath understands what that could feel like. Maybe you have a friend who is always asking things of you – money, a ride, your time. They are needy to the absolute maximum of your patience. They take and they take until you feel drained in every sense of the word.

I think Jesus must feel that way sometimes about us.

But He always listens, always gives, always provides, always loves, always pours himself out…even unto death on a cross. We need to do the same. We need to be open and willing to give and give until we can give no more. We need to model the heart of Christ and responding to a world that acts out of anger by reacting with love.

James 2:1-3 *"Therefore if there is any consolation in Christ, if any comfort of love, if any fellowship of the Spirit, if any affection and mercy, fulfill my joy by being like-minded, having the same love, being of one accord, of one mind."*

So, stop doing what you have always done, and start being of one mind with the ONE who wants to change your perspective to match His.

It does not make sense to us – but it works. Love works. Forgiveness works. Peace Works

NOTES

Introduction to Matthew Chapter 6

This chapter is summed up incredibly effectively in one verse of only two sentences. Matthew 6:1 says *"Be careful not to practice your righteousness in front of others to be seen by them. If you do, you will have no reward from your Father in heaven."*

After providing the roadmap with beatitudes, Jesus showed how we as Christians should behave towards others with topics like adultery, divorce, lying, and loving our enemies.

However, in Matthew Chapter 6 we see Jesus become a little introspective. He begins teaching some of the major disciplines that He is asking us as His followers to practice, such as prayer, fasting, giving to the poor. He focuses not only on what to do in these situations in a practical way, but what heart posture we should take in our spirit while we practice these things.

Here is a big secret to the Christian life – it is not for our own benefit. Jesus did not come to glorify Himself, but to glorify the Father. He does not ask us to live the Christian lifestyle for ourselves, but to build the Kingdom of God. We have said it before and it is a recurring theme throughout the Sermon, "seek first the Kingdom" and watch as the benefits to others and ourselves occur naturally.

This leads naturally to the topic of where we desire our treasures to be. Are we willing to trust our Father in Heaven to meet every single one of our needs for no other reason than He loves us and wants the best for His children?

Be prepared to turn your focus inward and examine your motives. I hope that you will see this as an opportunity to be and do better. To do what Jesus challenged us to do in the very last verse of Chapter 5, *"Be perfect, therefore, as your heavenly Father is perfect."*

10. Spiritual Integrity

"Be careful not to practice your righteousness in front of others to be seen by them. If you do, you will have no reward from your Father in heaven.

"So, when you give to the needy, do not announce it with trumpets, as the hypocrites do in the synagogues and on the streets, to be honored by others. Truly I tell you, they have received their reward in full. But when you give to the needy, do not let your left hand know what your right hand is doing, so that your giving may be in secret. Then your Father, who sees what is done in secret, will reward you.

"And when you pray, do not be like the hypocrites, for they love to pray standing in the synagogues and on the street corners to be seen by others. Truly I tell you, they have received their reward in full. But when you pray, go into your room, close the door, and pray to your Father, who is unseen. Then your Father, who sees what is done in secret, will reward you. And when you pray, do not keep on babbling like pagans, for they think they will be heard because of their many words. Do not be like them, for your Father knows what you need before you ask him."

"When you fast, do not look somber as the hypocrites do, for they disfigure their faces to show others they are fasting. Truly I tell you, they have received their reward in full. But when you fast, put oil on your head and wash your face, so that it will not be obvious to others that you are fasting, but only to your Father, who is unseen; and your Father, who sees what is done in secret, will reward you." (Matthew 6: 2-8, 16-18)

First, let me tell you that we will not be discussing the importance of giving to the less fortunate, prayer, or fasting. Why? If you are reading this, you already know that these three spiritual disciplines are important. If you do not, there are a ton of other books out there describing their importance in detail. What I want to discuss is the importance Jesus placed on how you behave when you are practicing these disciplines and WHY you practice them.

Prayer is vital to the Christian life and experience. The same can be said for fasting and giving to the less fortunate. However, just like every action that Jesus took on this planet – they are intended to glorify God and to edify the body. They are not, nor have they ever been for the purpose of making us look more spiritual. For years I was what some might call a spiritual skeptic. What I mean is that I believe that the Holy Spirit manifests itself in the world today but had a tough time buying in completely because I had seen far too many examples of people who "evidenced" the work of the Spirit to draw attention to themselves rather than to Jesus.

In the book *Shattering the Glass Slipper* by Charles Marshall, the author states that "Integrity is doing the right thing, even when no one is looking." Jesus tells those listening to his sermon to completely differentiate themselves from the religious leaders of the day by practicing these disciplines in secret, behind closed doors, and with no thought to their own reward. He even goes as far to say if they are recognized as practicing by others, that recognition is all the reward which will be given to them. Why do you think Jesus placed so much importance on doing things in secret? He says it several times, but you might have missed it. *"Then your Father, who sees what is done in secret, will reward you."*

When you take the importance of public recognition out of the equation and focus your attention on glorifying God and blessing and building up others, it leaves room for the Holy Spirit to move upon your behalf and reward you. Jesus was showing us an important aspect of God – his omnipresence. He is present everywhere – and sees when our hearts lead us to practice those things which bless His heart through our obedience to His Word.

The rewards of man are fleeting and of no substance, even if they make us feel temporarily important and recognized. The reward of heaven and the peace that only comes from God is more than enough to satisfy even the emptiest of heart. Best of all - they are eternal!

NOTES

11. There Is a Right Way to Do Things

"This then, is how you should pray: Our Father in heaven, hallowed be your name, your kingdom come, your will be done, on earth as it is in heaven. Give us today our daily bread. And forgive us our debts, as we also have forgiven our debtors. And lead us not into temptation but deliver us from the evil one. For if you forgive other people when they sin against you, your heavenly Father will also forgive you. But if you do not forgive others their sins, your Father will not forgive your sins." (Matthew 6: 9-13)

Let me say before I tell this story that I love my wife more than anything. She is my perfect compliment. Where I am weak, she shows strength. In our family, I am the cook. This is not because my wife cannot cook, it is because I love cooking, planning meals and providing them to friends and family. A common conversation occurs in our home regularly.

Me: "Honey, what do you want for dinner?"
Her: "Oh, whatever you want."
Me: "How about Spaghetti?"
Her: "No, I'm not really in the mood for Spaghetti."
Me: "How about Beef Stew?"
Her: "I'm not really feeling beef stew."
Me: "Well then, what would you like?"
Her: "Really honey, whatever you want to make is fine!"

I do not know whether you can relate to this specific situation, but I find that far too often in life people are easily able to tell us what NOT to do, but when it comes to telling us what to do, they are not as forthcoming.

Jesus had just finished telling his disciples and the crowd how not to pray like the hypocrites and not to babble on like pagans who just like to hear themselves talk. He then stated very clearly, "This, then, is how you should pray…" Jesus often told His followers the things to avoid because He did not want them falling into sin. However, He also never failed to point them, and us, in the right direction as well.

I have always admired people who can accomplish a lot with only a little. Jesus changed the world in only three years and finalized salvation for billions of people with three words, "It is finished." In these verses He enabled us to approach the throne of heaven and communicate with the almighty Creator of the universe with only fifty-three words. Imagine that!!!

The steps are easier than you might think.

Give God honor simply for WHO HE IS.

Ask for His will to be accomplished in our lives, and in the world around us.

Make our requests known for our needs. (Even though God knows our needs)

Ask forgiveness for the wrongs we have done and proclaim forgiveness for those who have wronged us.

Ask the Lord for protection against the works of the enemy in our world.

Then, Jesus restates something. I bring it to your attention because when someone repeats themselves, it is usually because it is important. Immediately after asking God for protection against the works of the evil one, Jesus tells us that if we forgive other people when they sin against us then God will forgive us. He also states that if we do not forgive others, we will not be forgiven our sins.

One of the greatest tools in the devil's arsenal is to breed division amongst the body of Christ. If we are so busy holding grudges and fighting each other, then our focus is off spreading the Kingdom of God. And how is it that we can truly approach the Lord in prayer if our hearts are clouded with bitterness or anger? To approach and attempt to communicate with the Lord while holding unforgiveness in our hearts is like trying to talk to someone through cans and a string when you have the latest cell phone in your pocket.

In John 17:22-23, Jesus prays to the Father, "*I have given them the glory that you gave me, that they may be one as we are one—I in them and you in me—so that they may be brought to complete unity. Then the world will know that you sent me and have loved them even as you have loved me.*"

The Kingdom of God is perfect unity. Unforgiveness cuts us off from every fruit the Spirit has to offer us. To truly give God honor – forgive. To truly see his Kingdom come and His will being done – forgive. To have Him truly supply your needs – forgive. To truly be protected from the works of the enemy – forgive.

Let the world know with absolute certainty that you are a follower of Jesus, and show you are glorifying God and building up the body of Christ by forgiving others, just as God has forgiven you.

There is not any miscommunication occurring here. Jesus is clearly telling you what to do – you should listen.

NOTES

12. What Are Your Priorities?

"Do not store up for yourselves treasures on earth, where moths and vermin destroy, and where thieves break in and steal. But store up for yourselves treasures in heaven, where moths and vermin do not destroy, and where thieves do not break in and steal. For where your treasure is, there your heart will be also.

"The eye is the lamp of the body. If your eyes are healthy, your whole body will be full of light. But if your eyes are unhealthy, your whole body will be full of darkness. If then the light within you is darkness, how great is that darkness!

"No one can serve two masters. Either you will hate the one and love the other, or you will be devoted to the one and despise the other. You cannot serve both God and money." (Matthew 6:19-24)

I do not know about any of you, but for most of my life there have been several things vying for my attention. As a little kid the choices were simple – do I play outside, do my chores, or finish my homework? Setting my priorities was not a challenging task at that time since my amazing mother made most of those choices for me.

As an adult it is not so easy. Adulting is hard. We must work because there are bills to pay. We need to find some sort of leisure activity, or we very well may lose what is left of our sanity. Being available for our spouse and children is a huge deal as family is where our morals and values are established and passed on to future generations as well as the place where we are supposed to experience security and unconditional love. Once you have children, there is even more pulling for attending. Everything from athletic and artistic lessons and activities to just making quality time with the kids. These add to an already very full plate.

But here is my question: Where does God fit in all of this? Where do our Creator and Savior fit on our priority list?

When my wife and I were dating and discussing what we were looking for in a partner, I was honest from the beginning that my priorities were simple: God, Family, everything else. What made me know that she was the one for me was that she spoke very clearly that I would always be second in her life behind her relationship with Jesus.

People everywhere forget that the very first list of rules laid down by God to Moses started with the what should be our first and frankly, our only priority – Exodus 20:1-3 "Then God gave the people all these instructions, "I am the Lord your God, who rescued you from the land of Egypt, the place of your slavery. You must not have any other god but me." God placed this as the first of the commandments because without making Him first in all things, the others become about simple obedience instead of us obeying Him out of our desire to glorify Him. God needs to be the absolute foundation of our lives for the rest of the levels to have any hope of standing.

In Matthew 22:37-40 Jesus told us that the greatest commandment was to, *"Love the Lord your God with all your heart and with all your soul and with all your mind. This is the first and greatest commandment. And the second is like it: 'Love your neighbor as yourself.' All the Law and the Prophets hang on these two commandments."* This shows that loving God should be and is the greatest priority in our lives. If all the laws and the words of the prophets hang on this commandment, it is important for us to make it a priority in our lives.

When Jesus was speaking of storing up treasures on earth over heaven, He was not speaking of money. He was speaking of our heart, mind, and soul. How many times in our lives have we spread ourselves so thin over so many things that nothing gets our FULL attention or energy. When our hearts and minds are focused on so many things, we are doing all of them a true disservice by not giving any of them our full attention.

When we place our treasures (heart, mind, soul) on things of earth, which are temporary, they will decay and die just like all temporal things. Jobs end, children grow up and move away, and marriages can end in divorce or spouses can pass away. There is only one area of our lives which is eternal – our relationship with the One who loves us and died for us.

When we place God above all else, the ultimate trickle-down effect takes place and permeates every area of our lives.

Do you want to strengthen your job and make it the best it can be? Place God at the center by working to be an example to your co-workers and pray for them and your place of employment.

Do you want to ensure that you have the strongest possible marriage? Place God at the center of it. Pray together as husband and wife. Worship together as husband and wife. Seek the very face of God together as husband and wife.

Do you want to genuinely love your children? Be an example of a walking the Christian life out to them. Pray WITH and FOR them. Worship with them. Forgive them when they screw up and always guide them towards a faith-based way of living.

Placing God at the center of your life is focusing your eyes in the right direction. Jesus tells us that our eyes are the lamp of the body, and by fixing our eyes on glorifying God and building the Kingdom fills our worlds with a light that will never end and grant to us rewards that "moths and vermin do not destroy and where thieves do not break in and steal." And when our eyes are filled with the light of God, it will impact every area of our lives.

Make God the priority and watch as all the others line right up. Matthew 6:33 - "Seek first His kingdom and His righteousness, and all these things will be given to you as well."

NOTES

13. God Knows Your Needs

"Therefore I tell you, do not worry about your life, what you will eat or drink; or about your body, what you will wear. Is not life more than food, and the body more than clothes? Look at the birds of the air; they do not sow or reap or store away in barns, and yet your heavenly Father feeds them. Are you not much more valuable than they? Can any one of you by worrying add a single hour to your life?

"And why do you worry about clothes? See how the flowers of the field grow. They do not labor or spin. Yet I tell you that not even Solomon in all his splendor was dressed like one of these. If that is how God clothes the grass of the field, which is here today and tomorrow is thrown into the fire, will he not much more clothe you—you of little faith? So do not worry, saying, 'What shall we eat?' or 'What shall we drink?' or 'What shall we wear?' For the pagans run after all these things, and your heavenly Father knows that you need them. But seek first his kingdom and his righteousness, and all these things will be given to you as well. Therefore, do not worry about tomorrow, for tomorrow will worry about itself. Each day has enough trouble of its own." (Matthew 6:25-34)

These ten short verses hit me directly in the heart. Often, when reading verses where Jesus describes certain behaviors, I easily can conclude that I am not guilty of them. However, when it comes to worrying, I am guilty as charged. See, my mother is a professional worrier. If there were an Olympics held celebrating people who could look at ANY SITUATION and see the negative possibilities that could occur, she would be the gold medalist in every event. It all comes from a place of love and genuine concern but just letting go and trusting is not her strong suit.

Unfortunately, I inherited a bit of that from her. I do not worry about some things. However, my one area where worry eats at my heart is one that I am sure is shared by many of you – money. I realize the irony that money is my area of worry, and I chose education and ministry as my areas of profession. Not exactly compatible for someone who wants a secure financial future, but still, there is a roof over my head, food on the table, my children are clothed, and my bills are paid. Yet, I still worry whether the next paycheck will be enough.

Why? Why do I worry when God has constantly and consistently shown that He has and will continue to provide for my needs? Is it a lack of faith? Disobedience? More importantly – why does Jesus specifically tell His followers and all who would follow not to worry. Why was it so important?

Because Jesus has a purpose for you to fulfill now. You were born for such a time as this. You were created not for tomorrow, but for now! I was told once as a child that if I am constantly focused on myself, I will never be able to see anything going on around me. When our minds are constantly clouded by worry, we are unable to focus on what is around us today, which Jesus tells us with the words, *"Therefore, do not worry about tomorrow, for tomorrow will worry about itself. Each day has enough trouble of its own."*

Worry is easily the most useless emotion that a human can experience. There is no good that can come from it. Jesus says it plainly, *"Can any one of you by worrying add a single hour to your life?"* Worrying about money does not fill my bank account. Worrying about disease will not stop cancer from occurring. Worrying about my kids will not protect them from a cruel world.

The Lord God is omnipotent, omniscient, and omnipresent Those are three big words that tell us that God is all-powerful, all-knowing, and always with us no matter where we may go. If

God is always with us, He is aware of the circumstances around us. If God is all-knowing, then He knows our needs before we ever speak them. If God is all-powerful, then as it says in Philippians 4:19, He can and will *"meet all your needs according to the riches of his glory in Christ Jesus."*

These verses in Chapter 6 were not intended to chastise the Jews for worrying. Jesus is trying to get two particularly important points across.

Every single one of us has TREMENDOUS value to our Father in heaven. God created every bird and flower and feeds and cares for them, but Jesus tells us plainly that we are more valuable. If anything tells you that you are valuable, it is the knowledge that God gave up His Son so He could be with YOU forever.

If we keep our focus on what is important, these worldly things will never trouble our mind. After 41 years of faith in God and 26 years of ministry, I find it hard to believe that there are any words in the entire Bible that more clearly state where we as Christians should place our entire focus than Matthew 6:33, "Seek first His kingdom and His righteousness, and all these things will be given to you as well."

When we follow this command to Seek His kingdom and righteousness first, we are given the opportunity to see miracles occur right before our eyes. We can witness the lost being found and restored to new life in Jesus. When we are a witness to these miracles, it can do nothing but increase our faith that the very same God who is restoring the lost loves us and wants nothing but good things for his children. We will still face troubles, but we have a God who became flesh and overcame the world. This same all-powerful God will always care for those who call upon His name.

So, stop worrying – and start seeking Him.

NOTES

Introduction to Matthew Chapter 7

Matthew 7 is a chapter that really forces the reader (or listener) to think hard. Jesus starts discussing some difficult subjects and asks those who follow Him to search within themselves to find the truth that lies at the heart of His words.

Talk about some meat to chew on. Judging others, doing unto others as you would have them do unto you, false prophets as well as false disciples, and building our houses on a foundation of rock.

These words made heads spin in that time, and they continue to do so today. Jesus was not afraid of difficult topics, and he asked that we do the same. He wants us to mull these words over in our minds repeatedly until we gain the understanding that will come once we start to consider them not only with our minds, but our hearts.

Sometimes it is hard for us to truly grasp how revolutionary his words were. Do not judge people? That is crazy. Of course we should judge bad people for terrible acts. Ask and it will be given to you? Imagine saying them to a generation of Israelites who had been begging for God to rescue them from the Romans. Wide and narrow roads? False prophets and good and bad fruit? Then to top it all off, telling them directly that not everyone will enter the Kingdom of Heaven.

I want to admit something to you that does not come easy for me to say. Sometimes I like to instigate people just to start a discussion. I enjoy debate, argument, or whatever words you want to call it. I like the free exchange of ideas and hammering my point across. Jesus was not arguing here. He placed the questions in the minds of the people so that they would have the argument and understanding grow within their own heads and hearts. He spoke these absolute truths in the face of a society that argued against all of it, and he did so with authority.

He knew what would happen as a result. He knew that He was inviting the Pharisees and teachers of the law to challenge Him. He knew that this message would spread throughout the world and as a result, He could no longer be ignored or overlooked. This message would bring Him into direct conflict with the authorities and result in His arrest and death. He preached the message anyway.

I hope these chapters do the same for you. I pray that after reading them, you can no longer overlook Christ and His message for you.

14. First Things First

"Do not judge, or you too will be judged. For in the same way you judge others, you will be judged, and with the measure you use, it will be measured to you.

"Why do you look at the speck of sawdust in your brother's eye and pay no attention to the plank in your own eye? How can you say to your brother, 'Let me take the speck out of your eye,' when all the time there is a plank in your own eye? You hypocrite, first take the plank out of your own eye, and then you will see clearly to remove the speck from your brother's eye.

"Do not give dogs what is sacred; do not throw your pearls to pigs. If you do, they may trample them under their feet and turn and tear you to pieces." (Matthew 7:1-6)

Welcome to what might be the single most incorrectly used scripture ever. Hundreds of people who attempt to stay in their lives of sin have turned this into a motto. Maybe you have heard its more popular version, "Only God can judge me."

This may surprise you, but I agree with them completely. It is not our purpose to judge anyone. It is not our responsibility to condemn anyone for their words, actions, or deeds. I also agree with them with the fact that God will indeed judge them. However, I wish they would realize what a frightening prospect that is.

Here's where things get confusing for some people. As Christians, we are told we are to imitate Christ in all things, and one thing that Jesus did was bring people's sins to light. Here is the difference – when Jesus pointed out sins there was no judgment, only forgiveness. When he healed the paralytic who was lowered through the roof, he said your sins are forgiven. When he met the woman at the well, he pointed out her multiple husbands and that she was living in sin and then he offered her a drink of living water.

Well, if we are supposed to follow Jesus' example, shouldn't we point out the sin in others? Jesus tells us that if we are going to point out the speck in our brother's eye (his sin) then we need to go and remove the plank from our own eye (our sin) so we can see clearly to HELP our brother. I hope you see the difference. The reason Jesus can reach out and pluck the sins from our eye is HE HAD NO SINS. He can discern the hearts of people and forgive, allowing them to "go and sin no more."

I do not know you, but I am almost certain that you have sinned – even today. I am also sure that you do not have the ability to forgive sins (only Jesus can do that). The Holy Spirit may give you the ability to discern the spirit within people and see a sinful heart, but what that means is that we have even more of a responsibility to point that person to the ONE that can truly clear their hearts of sin, Jesus. The only motive which should ever influence our hearts when approaching others about their sin is the desire to restore them to their heavenly Father.

The final part of these verses tells us "*Do not give dogs what is sacred; do not throw your pearls to pigs. If you do, they may trample them under their feet and turn and tear you to pieces.*" Jesus had just finished telling us to practice self-examination and discernment when dealing with those who sin. He wanted us to practice this with our relationships. We are not to give our gifts to those who have no desire to honor them but will only turn and trash them. Christ desires for us to protect our hearts. Here is the thing about pigs – they will eat anything. They have no care about the quality of what they are eating. They care only to consume it entirely. If we give the gift of our heart, soul, and mind to the pigs of this world we take the chance to lose it entirely.

Jesus also tells us not to give dogs what is sacred. In 2 Peter 2:21-22 it says *"It would have been better for them not to have known the way of righteousness, than to have known it and then to turn their backs on the sacred command that was passed on to them. Of them the proverbs are true: "A dog returns to its vomit."* The thing about dogs is that they can indeed be friendly and loyal, but they do not grasp the value of things.

I have three amazing dogs, and I love them more than anything outside of my wife and kids. There is nothing in the world that can turn my stomach faster than when they eat too quickly or eat something they should not and end up throwing it up and then attempting to eat it. Here is the thing – they do not know any better. They do not understand that what they are trying to do will hurt them because they are simply putting their fleshly desire for food above what is best for them.

People do the same. We have all known people who have escaped sin and then returned to it. They may have even fully been walking with God for a time only to turn their back when they become hurt or offended. Jesus tells us not to place our sacred trust in people who behave as dogs – those who will simply care more for the desires of the flesh than joy of the Spirit we try to share with them. Practice discernment to always put the Spirit before the flesh – first things first.

When living a Christian life, we must walk that life out with discernment. Not only to lead others back to the arms of God, but also to protect our own salvation and witness!

NOTES

15. It Really Is not Complicated

"Ask and it will be given to you; seek and you will find; knock and the door will be opened to you. For everyone who asks receives; the one who seeks finds; and to the one who knocks, the door will be opened.

"Which of you, if your son asks for bread, will give him a stone? Or if he asks for a fish, will give him a snake? If you, then, though you are evil, know how to give good gifts to your children, how much more will your Father in heaven give good gifts to those who ask him! So, in everything, do to others what you would have them do to you, for this sums up the Law and the Prophets."

"Enter through the narrow gate. For wide is the gate and broad is the road that leads to destruction, and many enter through it. [14] But small is the gate and narrow the road that leads to life, and only a few find it." (Matthew 7:7-12)

My first job following college was as the Director of Youth Ministries at First United Methodist Church of Maumelle, Arkansas. First, let me say that at only twenty-two years of age I had absolutely no business being a youth pastor. I did not possess the maturity or common sense to lead much of anything. God used me despite my shortcomings and the twenty months I spent at that position were some of the most amazing times of ministry I have ever experienced. I forged lifelong friendships as a result.

One evening in November, I had the entire youth group follow me outside and we just sat on the lawn and sidewalk beside the parking lot. Now it may not get as cold in Arkansas, but it was a little chilly. We sat there in absolute silence. We were not talking, singing, or preaching. We just sat there. I could tell the students (about eighty all together) were confused and uncomfortable, but no one said a thing. After about fifteen minutes of staring at each other, one of my seniors named Katie said, "I have a cross-country meet tomorrow and I cannot afford to get sick, can we please go back inside?" I smiled and said, "Of course, all you had to do was ask."

Why do we make things so much more difficult than they have to be? Maybe you are so sanctified that you have no clue what I am talking about, but for most people, this is a common occurrence in MOST areas of our lives. Allow me to let you in on a little secret – Loving God and receiving what He has for you is not complicated.

Jesus shows us just how simple it is, "Ask and it will be given to you; seek and you will find; knock and the door will be opened to you. For everyone who asks receives; the one who seeks finds; and to the one who knocks, the door will be opened." If you want the blessings of God, ask for them. If you want the fruit of the Spirit in your life, SEEK that fruit. The Lord WANTS to give good gifts to His children. His desire is for you to operate in your gifts and calling and for you to walk with Him. He has given us every tool we need to make that happen.

"So, in everything, do to others what you would have them do to you, for this sums up the Law and the Prophets." There is one other place where Jesus says that the law and prophets hang on something.

Matthew 22:37-40 *"Love the Lord your God with all your heart and with all your soul and with all your mind.' This is the first and greatest commandment. And the second is like it: 'Love your neighbor as yourself.' All the Law and the Prophets hang on these two commandments."* These two moments let me know something that Jesus makes clear – Loving God and loving your neighbor is shown and evidenced by doing to others what we would have them do to us. That is not complicated. Love God and love people. The heart of the entire gospel, and the Kingdom of God is founded entirely upon loving God and loving people. IT'S NOT COMPLICATED.

It is man who complicates things. Jesus left this earth with a simple command in Matthew 28 19-20, *"Therefore go and make disciples of all nations, baptizing them in the name of the Father and of the Son and of the Holy Spirit, and teaching them to obey everything I have commanded you. And surely, I am with you always, to the very end of the age."*

Then man comes in and complicates things. "Baptize them in the name of the Father and of the Son and of the Holy Spirit" Sure thing, but only if you are dunking them…don't you dare sprinkle or pour the water. "Obey everything I have commanded you." Okay, but make sure you follow our rule book while you are doing it. Man constantly and consistently changes and adjusts and, frankly, ruins what was originally beautifully made by God.

According to the Center for the Study of Global Christianity at Gordon-Cromwell Theological Seminary, there are over two hundred Christian denominations in the US alone and over 45,000 globally. What started as a unified movement with a unified purpose has fractured and morphed into something divided and complicated beyond belief. When did the mission of Christ become so complicated?

John 17:20-23 *"My prayer is not for them alone. I pray also for those who will believe in me through their message, that all of them may be one, Father, just as you are in me, and I am in you. May they also be in us so that the world may believe that you have sent me. I have given them the glory that you gave me, that they may be one as we are one— I in them and you in me—so that they may be brought to complete unity. Then the world will know that you sent me and have loved them even as you have loved me."*

God desires UNITY. And how do we become unified? It is simple….

Love God – Love People.
Glorify God – Edify the Body.

We do not even have to worry about knowing HOW to do these things. *"Enter through the narrow gate. For wide is the gate and broad is the road that leads to destruction, and many enter through it. But small is the gate and narrow the road that leads to life, and only a few find it."* This may seem like Jesus is saying that the road is more difficult to travel, but what He is saying to me is that the route we are asked to travel is DIRECT. The gate is small and the way narrow because, as it says in Matthew 22:14, *"Many are called, but few are chosen."* The wide, broad path to destruction must be that way because way too many people choose that path.

We have a huge advantage, though, as God has given us the perfect example of walking the narrow way because Jesus walked it before and lived the perfect example of how to do it, and He left us the Holy Spirit to "guide you into all truth." (John 16:13)

Love God – Love People

Glorify God – Edify the Body

It is not complicated – so do not let the world make it complicated. Stay close to the ONE who made it simple and will continue to simplify things for you if you ask, seek, and knock.

NOTES

16. Things Are not Always What They Seem

"Watch out for false prophets. They come to you in sheep's clothing, but inwardly they are ferocious wolves. By their fruit you will recognize them. Do people pick grapes from thornbushes, or figs from thistles? Likewise, every good tree bears good fruit, but a bad tree bears bad fruit. A good tree cannot bear bad fruit, and a bad tree cannot bear good fruit. Every tree that does not bear good fruit is cut down and thrown into the fire. Thus, by their fruit you will recognize them."

"Not everyone who says to me, 'Lord, Lord,' will enter the kingdom of heaven, but only the one who does the will of my Father who is in heaven. Many will say to me on that day, 'Lord, Lord, did we not prophesy in your name and in your name drive out demons and, in your name, perform many miracles?' Then I will tell them plainly, 'I never knew you. Away from me, you evildoers!'" (Matthew 7:15-23)

I am sure that many of you are familiar with the phrase, "If it walks like a duck and quacks like a duck, then it must be a duck." The phrase is a proverb that is intended to show that we can identify something by observing its natural state and characteristics. The irony is that the phrase originated from an event in 1738 when a Frenchman named Jacques de Vaucanson invented a *mechanical* duck which could quack, waddle, eat food, and would appear to digest that food and produce a mixture that looked and smelled like duck droppings. It may have looked, acted, and sounded like the real thing – but the result was still completely fake.

Jesus shows us in Matthew 7:15-23 that we will see some impressive forgeries while walking the path of faith. They will dress the part and spout scripture from memory. They will sing the songs and raise their hands in "worship" and speak *"Christian-ese"* fluently. They may even have a testimony that brings us to tears and some may even experience manifestations and miracles in their services and meetings. The façade will be big and impressive and seem so real.

But what fruit do they bear? Jesus is adamant that you will know those "false prophets" by their fruits. First let me tell you that even though many judge the success of a ministry by the size of their offerings, the number of people in a congregation, their online following, or the number of people wearing their merchandise. However, the fruits of a ministry have nothing to do with these things.

The fruits which a true, God-fearing, and God-following ministry will bear are found in Galatians 5:22-23, *"But the Holy Spirit produces this kind of fruit in our lives: love, joy, peace, patience, kindness, goodness, faithfulness, gentleness, and self-control. There is no law against these things!"* (NLT)

Many times, in my journey as a Christian, I have experienced what I thought were real moments during church services, concerts, and relationships with "spiritual" people that ended with none of the fruits being evidenced in my life or in the lives of those who were with me. If you leave your encounter with one of these so called "prophets" and there is no love or joy flowing through you, or any of the other fruits increasing in your spirit as a result, then it is a safe bet that what you thought was real was merely a mirage.

The next part of Jesus' message is the one that not only gives me pause when choosing where I worship with my family but gives me pause when I endeavor to use my giftings in Jesus' name. *"Not everyone who says to me, 'Lord, Lord,' will enter the kingdom of heaven, but only the one who does the will of my Father who is in heaven. Many will say to me on that day, 'Lord, Lord, did we not prophesy in your name and in your name drive out demons and, in your name, perform many miracles?' Then I will tell them plainly, 'I never knew you. Away from me, you evildoers!'"*

It is difficult to describe, but the best way I can interpret what this is telling me is that when it comes to walking the Christian life is that talk is cheap. How easy is it to say the words that make us look and seem spiritual? We have seen the rise and fall of so many well-known "preachers" over the years who could talk the talk of Christianity but whose lives showed that they never let the words come to life in their hearts.

My undergraduate degree was in vocal performance and composition. All that means is that I spent a lot of scholarship money for four years learning to sing and write music. (Yes, I am aware that was not the most economically sound choice). However, I had to take a course called "diction" where I learned to pronounce many of the different classical languages that choral music is written in – Latin, French, etc. I can pronounce the words but have no earthly idea what I am saying when I do.

The same thing occurs in the church. People memorize the prayers but never let them sink in. They know all the right words to say. They know how to make their voice rise and fall and drip with emotion, but their hearts remain empty. Jesus tells us plainly that not everyone who simply speaks the words will enter the kingdom. He tells us that it must go beyond the words to DOING the will of the Father – Loving God and Loving people. He goes even further that there will even be people who prophesy and cast out demons and perform miracles, but because they do not really know Jesus intimately, they will not enter the kingdom. How can we tell if someone knows Jesus? By their fruits. Now, wait a minute. Are you saying that miracles like casting out demons and prophesying are not fruits? Yes, that is exactly what I am saying. They may be manifestations of the spirit, but they are not fruits.

The magicians in Pharaoh's court were able to imitate some of the signs that Moses did, but it was NOT the result of God's presence. Miracles and manifestations are often used to gain the attention of non-believers, but their purpose should ALWAYS draw attention to the Father, not to the things of man.

The outstanding music group Shane and Shane have a song titled "Without Jesus" that says it better than I ever could…

"You can memorize, become a Mennonite.
You can speak in tongues and bring the dead to life.
You could build a big church, call it ministry
Teach 'em all they need to know to run a family
You could sell it all, be burned at the stake
But what in the world have you to ever gain
Without Jesus?"

1 Corinthians 13: 1-3 says it even better, *"If I speak in the tongues of men or of angels, but do not have love, I am only a resounding gong or a clanging cymbal. If I have the gift of prophecy and can fathom all mysteries and all knowledge, and if I have a faith that can move mountains, but do not have love, I am nothing. If I give all I possess to the poor and give over my body to hardship that I may boast, but do not have love, I gain nothing."*

As believers, our goal is to love God and love people and as a result build the kingdom of God. To discern the difference between those who walk this same path from those who seek only personal gain you must look to the fruits – the greatest of which is love. All the miracles and manifestations in the world added together mean nothing without love.

If we desire to spread God's kingdom, then we must show the evidence that we know Jesus intimately. What evidence can show we are the real thing? John 13:35 *"By this everyone will know that you are my disciples, if you love one another."*

Remember, talk is cheap. If you desire to change the world for the kingdom of God, make sure you are exactly what you seem to be. Show how much you love Jesus by loving each other.

NOTES

17. Location, Location, Location

> *"Therefore everyone who hears these words of mine and puts them into practice is like a wise man who built his house on the rock. The rain came down, the streams rose, and the winds blew and beat against that house; yet it did not fall, because it had its foundation on the rock. But everyone who hears these words of mine and does not put them into practice is like a foolish man who built his house on sand. The rain came down, the streams rose, and the winds blew and beat against that house, and it fell with a great crash."* (Matthew 7: 24-27)

Recently, I have begun looking towards the future. I am at an age where retirement is much closer than I am comfortable with and the idea of spending my golden years in a location where my feet can be in the ocean every evening seems pretty darn appealing. So, I have begun spending more time than I am happy to admit searching real estate sites and have noticed something.... houses at the beach are astronomically more expensive than houses here in little old West Virginia. The same house there is a minimum of **two hundred thousand dollars** more expensive than it is here. Why? Location.

Location is everything. Being near the best schools, shopping places, entertainment, landmarks, churches and even being near the local bus line can change the price of a home. The location of a home has everything to do with the value placed on and the price associated with living there.

The life you live is the same. Your location matters. Where you place yourself matters. Where you choose to build influences the value of your life and influences the price associated with living it. The wise man chooses to build where his life has the greatest value. Now where would that be? John 15:9-13 says that *"As the Father has loved me, so have I loved you. Now remain in my love. If you keep my commands, you will remain in my love, just as I have kept my Father's commands and remain in his love. I have told you this so that my joy may be in you and that your joy may be complete. My command is this: Love each other as I have loved you. Greater love has no one than this: to lay down one's life for one's friends."* We find our greatest value when we remain in the love of Christ. How do we show that we have remained in His love? By the love we show for others.

Everyone builds a life for themselves. Everyone puts together a combination of people, places, things, emotions, and events which create their world. You can think of this world as a house with each room painstakingly arranged and decorated to make sure it maximizes some aspects of their personality. Everyone's house is different. Everyone's house is personalized for them.

Maybe you are the housebuilder that wants an open concept where every room flows into the other. Maybe you want a retro feel where you allow the past to influence your present circumstances. Maybe you are like me where the kitchen needs to be the focus of your house because food means fellowship and family. One thing that all houses have in common no matter what size, shape, or age is that without a solid foundation, it will not stand.

Jesus tells us to build our home on a foundation made of rock so it will stand when the rains come, and the winds blow. He also lets us know with absolute clarity how to do this, *"Therefore everyone who hears these words of mine and puts them into practice is like a wise man who built his house on the rock."*

The one, true way to build our house on the foundation of Christ is to put the words of Christ into practice. We must begin walking out what we have learned. We must take all we have learned in this sermon on the mount and LIVE IT. For people who are familiar with recovery, you can call this the twelve steps to living the Christian life.

We must:

Be the salt of the earth and light of the world by standing out and representing God's love.

Forgive our brothers and then approach God with our gifts.

Learn to let our yes be yes and our no be no and to love others sacrificially.

Love our enemies and pray for those who persecute us.

Live out the spiritual disciplines of prayer, fasting, and charity with humility and only to lead others to Jesus.

Place our heart and focus on God and not the things of this world.

Trust in God to meet all our needs and seek His kingdom first in all things.

Love others enough to gently point out the sin in their lives to reconcile them to the Father.

Do not be afraid to ask God for the desires of your heart and always approach and treat others with love.

Tread the narrow way as one chosen by God and use discernment to distinguish the false prophets which threaten God's children.

Make sure to know Jesus intimately and remain in His love.

And finally, build your life on a foundation of Worship, Prayer, and feasting on the Word.

This foundation can withstand anything the world can throw at you. John 16:33 *"I have told you these things, so that in me you may have peace. In this world you will have trouble. But take heart! I have overcome the world."* Jesus did not say that our foundations would stand IF the rains and winds come. He said WHEN. However, choosing every day to love God and love people enables you to bear the fruit of the Spirit in the midst of the storm.

There is a reason that Jesus' last words to His disciples before He ascended to the Father were of comfort. Matthew 28:20 *"And surely I am with you always, to the very end of the age."* He said it because He knew we would need him every day of our lives. That building our homes and lives on the foundation of Jesus' love would be the only way we would stand, and He tells us we will.

The foundation comes first. Seek first His kingdom and righteousness. His kingdom is easy to see and explain. It is all about loving God and loving people. That is the rock that we must build our home, life, and faith upon.

NOTES

18. All Authority

"When Jesus had finished saying these things, the crowds were amazed at his teaching, ²⁹ because he taught as one who had authority, and not as their teachers of the law." (Matthew 7:28-29)

I am consistently amazed at these last words of Matthew 7. Matthew was watching and writing what he had seen and felt it was important to point out that people were amazed not by what He had said, but because he was saying these things with authority. These things he said were new and unfamiliar. The Jews had been living through the oppression of Rome and had longed for a Messiah for centuries yet here Jesus was telling them to love and pray for the ones persecuting them. Yet, instead of being offended, they were amazed because He spoke with authority.

Let us go back to the beginning of the sermon where people followed Him because they had witnessed Jesus traveling throughout Galilee healing the sick, casting out demons, opening blinded eyes, and helping the paralyzed to walk. Even with these miracles, the people were AMAZED at his authority, which they specifically said was unlike the other teachers of the law.

What did Jesus have that the other teachers did not? We can pass over the obvious thing that He was, in fact, one with God and go to the one the people did not know about yet. He spoke with authority because He was living and would continue to live His words out every day to everyone. Jesus lived and walked by example.

He was a servant leader with no thought to His own acclaim. In fact, the Bible tells us in Philippians 2:7 that *"rather, he made himself nothing by taking the very nature of a servant, being made in human likeness."* He did not view the people He was speaking to as subjects to control, but as family who needed to be reconciled to their Father. He lived and acted with only ONE desire, to bring glory to the Father and to love people. Restoration and atonement. Sound familiar?

I have a life verse. 1 Corinthians 2:1-5 *"And so it was with me, brothers and sisters. When I came to you, I did not come with eloquence or human wisdom as I proclaimed to you the testimony about God. For I resolved to know nothing while I was with you except Jesus Christ and him crucified. I came to you in weakness with great fear and trembling. My message and my preaching were not with wise and persuasive words, but with a demonstration of the Spirit's power, so that your faith might not rest on human wisdom, but on God's power."*

I live by this verse because I cannot change anyone. Any wisdom or gifting I have is a direct result of walking with Jesus and trusting in HIS power. The same will be said of anyone who claims to live for the Lord. Galatians 2:20 tells us that, "I have been crucified with Christ and I no longer live, but Christ lives in me. The life I now live in the body, I live by faith in the Son of God, who loved me and gave himself for me."

The authority with which Jesus spoke came from the fact that the Father and He were one. Any authority with which we speak comes when we become one with the Holy Spirit when he takes up residence within us at our salvation moment. Jesus never lived for Himself. He held no desire other than to do the Father's will. He only lived to build the Kingdom by glorifying the Father and loving His children.

When we make building the kingdom OUR goal. When we make it the absolute foundation of our life. When we "Seek first the kingdom of God and His righteousness" then we can walk in the authority of Christ. We can lead others to an awesome truth–that the God of the universe loves them and desires a real, eternal relationship with them. This authority amazed the crowds that day, and if we let it, it can still amaze us just as much today.

NOTES

One Last Word from the Author...

In 26 years of ministry people often will come to me and ask me where to start when it comes to reading the Bible and studying what it means to be a Christian. I used to point them to James or Romans because they focus on practical instructions for the Christian life and are easier to understand that some of the other books.

But allow me to say that from this moment forward, I will forever point new Christians to Matthew 5-7 and the Sermon on the Mount. Jesus' first full declaration of the purpose and truth of his ministry would seem to hold significant importance. Firsts usually do. First words, first steps, first love, etc.

These three chapters dive deeply into the heart of God and the desire to be reconciled with His children, and that heart and desire has not changed in the two thousand years since He gave the sermon. It points to the ultimate purpose of Christ and the purpose of the Christian walk.

I know I have said it a lot, but it bears repeating. Matthew 6:33 *"But seek first his kingdom and his righteousness, and all these things will be given to you as well."* And this kingdom is founded on loving God and loving people. Period. It does not get any simpler than that.

So, trust this roadmap that Jesus laid out for us. Let it teach you, chastise you, and amaze you. Let it point you to the goal of the gospel and let it CHANGE YOU from the inside out.

Then, let it guide you to others who need that change as well. Love God…. Love People.

www.ingramcontent.com/pod-product-compliance
Lightning Source LLC
LaVergne TN
LVHW011214080426
835508LV00007B/791